Contents

Words printed in bold letters, **like these**, are explained in the Glossary. Japanese judo terms printed in italics, *like these*, are explained on page 45.

The techniques in this book are described as they would be performed by a right-sided fighter. Many fighters, though, are left-sided, and they would perform the same techniques by twisting to the right, for example, rather than the left.

An Olympic final

Sydney, 22 September 2000: The Olympic judo competition was drawing to a close, but the arena was still packed with spectators. They were waiting for one of the most eagerly anticipated contests of the entire Games. The final of the men's heavyweight competition was about to begin. On one side was David Douillet of France; on the other, Shinichi Shinohara of Japan.

A clash of two giants

Douillet had already won two Olympic medals: a bronze in 1992, and then a gold at the Atlanta games in 1996. Shortly after Atlanta, Douillet was involved in a serious motorbike accident. He recovered from his injuries to return to competition and win the 1997 world championships, beating Shinohara in the final. The win was controversial, as it came from a penalty given against Shinohara by a French judge. Controversy was to haunt the 2000 Olympic final too.

In 1999, a back injury stopped Douillet from taking part in the world championships. At these championships Shinohara won ten of his eleven fights by *ippon* – a decisive score – and took both the heavyweight and open crowns. The stage was set for an almighty clash between two giants of the judo world.

Ninety seconds into the 2000 Olympic final Douillet launched an attack, trying to throw Shinohara. But Shinohara twisted away from the throw – both fighters hit the mat, Douillet landing on his back. The referee raised his arm to indicate a minor score, *yuko*, for Douillet. The crowd looked to the judges. One seemed to indicate that Shinohara had won by *ippon*. The other seemed to agree with the referee. Finally, Douillet was awarded *yuko*.

In the end, only this minor score separated the two fighters. The Japanese team manager (Yasuhiro Yamashita, a judo legend who had won gold at the 1984 Los Angeles Games) launched a protest.

Shinohara throws an opponent during the 1997 world championships. That year, he lost in the final to Douillet.

The Making of a Champion

A World-Class Judo Champion

Paul Mason

www.heinemann.co.uk/library
Visit our website to find out more information about **Heinemann Library** books.

To order:
☎ Phone 44 (0) 1865 888066
🖷 Send a fax to 44 (0) 1865 314091
💻 Visit the Heinemann Bookshop at www.heinemann.co.uk/library to browse our catalogue and order online.

First published in Great Britain by Heinemann Library, Halley Court, Jordan Hill, Oxford OX2 8EJ, part of Harcourt Education. Heinemann is a registered trademark of Harcourt Education Ltd.

© Harcourt Education Ltd 2004
First published in paperback in 2005
The moral right of the proprietor has been asserted.

Editorial: Andrew Farrow and Dan Nunn
Design: David Poole and Geoff Ward
Illustrations: Geoff Ward
Picture Research: Rebecca Sodergren and Fiona Orbell
Production: Viv Hichens

Originated by Ambassador Litho Ltd
Printed in China by WKT Company Limited

ISBN 0 431 18925 0 (hardback)
08 07 06 05 04
10 9 8 7 6 5 4 3 2 1

ISBN 0 431 18932 3 (paperback)
09 08 07 06 05
10 9 8 7 6 5 4 3 2 1

British Library Cataloguing in Publication Data
Mason, Paul
A World-Class Judo Player - (The Making of a Champion)
1. Judo - Juvenile literature
2. Judo - Training - Juvenile literature
I. Title
796.8'152
A full catalogue record for this book is available from the British Library.

Acknowledgements
The publishers would like to thank the following for permission to reproduce photographs:

Action Plus pp. **12**, **15 bottom**; Alamy p. **33** (David Hoffman Photo Library); Bob Willingham pp. **4**, **6 top**, **7**, **8**, **9 top**, **10**, **11**, **13 top**, **13 bottom**, **16**, **17 bottom**, **18 left**, **18 right**, **19**, **20 (x 6)**, **21**, **22**, **23**, **28**, **29**, **30**, **31 top**, **31 bottom**, **34**, **35**, **38**, **41**; Corbis pp. **5 top** (Jacques Langevin/Sygma), **5 bottom** (Jacques Langevin/Sygma), **27 top**; Empics pp. **6 bottom** (DPA), **15 top** (Tony Marshall), **17 top** (Matthew Ashton), **36**, **42** (Sygma/Hekimian Julien), **43 top** (Prevosto Olivier); L'Equipe pp. **14**, **37**; Getty News and Sport p. **27 bottom** (Stanley Chou/Allsport); Harcourt Education p. **9 bottom** (Trevor Clifford); Reuters pp. **24** (Kimimasa Mayama), **25 bottom** (Jack Dabaghian), **39** (Kimimasa Mayama), **43 bottom** (Philippe Wojazer); Rex Features/Sipa Press p. **25 top**; SPL p. **32** (John Heseltine); Unknown p. **40**.

Cover photograph reproduced with permission of Bob Willingham.

But the result stood: Douillet had managed to win a second gold, and promptly retired from international judo competition. Shinohara was inconsolable, and cried throughout the medal ceremony.

A controversial ending

The decision in this bout was a close one, and the judges at the side of the mat did not have the advantage of endless TV replays. Most people now agree that neither fighter should have been awarded a score. But no matter how controversial, all judo fighters have to abide by the decision of the judges.

Douillet and Shinohara, pictured airborne during their fight at the 2000 Olympic judo final.

Olympic judo fact

Until David Douillet's victory in 2000, no fighter had ever won judo medals at three different Olympic Games.

Douillet raises his arms in triumph after taking gold at Sydney while, to the right, Shinohara looks distraught.

The roots of judo

Judo grew out of a Japanese fighting style called ju-jitsu. Ju-jitsu includes techniques that use short weapons – stabbing and slashing, for example – as well as weaponless techniques such as hitting, kicking and choking. Ju-jitsu was adapted by a man named Jigoro Kano, who founded the fighting style called Kodokan Judo in 1882.

One of the few photos of Jigoro Kano of Japan, who invented judo in 1882. His sport has since spread around the whole world.

Early competition

The first *dojo* (judo practice area) had just nine students, but the sport grew rapidly. In 1886 the Tokyo police held a tournament between Kodokan Judo fighters and one of the most famous ju-jitsu schools, the Totsuka. Judo fighters drew two fights and won the other thirteen. By 1888, judo had been adopted as the official system of self-defence for the Tokyo police.

Judo in the Olympics

Judo's popularity spread throughout the 20th century. In 1964 the Olympic Games were held in Tokyo, Japan and judo medals were awarded for the first time. Back then there were three weight categories (light, middle and heavyweight) and competition was open only to men. Women's judo first appeared at the Olympics in 1988, when it was a **demonstration sport** at the Seoul Games. In 1992 women's medals were awarded for the first time, and women's judo has been a part of the Games ever since.

Here Anton Geesink of the Netherlands is pictured defeating Koji Sone of Japan, to win gold at the 1961 world championships in the men's open division. Geesink was the first non-Japanese judoka to win a title, and went on to take gold at the 1964 Olympics.

The spirit of judo

Judo is sometimes known as 'the gentle way', although to anyone who has just been on the wrong end of a winning throw it feels anything but gentle. It got this unusual name because judo is based on the idea of using an opponent's force against them, which is more 'gentle' than using your own power alone. Judo has its own character, which is very different from football or basketball, for example, where players may sometimes argue with referees and coaches. Judo students must listen carefully to their instructors and try hard to follow their advice. Above all, every fighter is expected to show the sport as a whole – including other fighters, coaches, judges and officials – complete respect.

Women's contests are every bit as competitive as men's. This is Sharon Rendle of the UK (left) performing a shoulder throw at the world championships in Paris, 1997.

'Traditional' versus 'wrestling' styles

Today, two main styles of judo exist. The first is the 'traditional' style, which has developed from the techniques of Jigoro Kano. It is reasonably upright, and uses gripping on the opponent's jacket as an important part of the technique. The second style developed in countries that were formerly part of the **Soviet bloc**, and is sometimes called the 'Russian' or 'wrestling' style. This developed partly from traditional wrestling techniques, and uses jacket grips far less. Some wrestling-style fighters even train without their jacket on.

Champion fact

The first-ever women's world judo champion was Jane Bridge of England in November 1980, who fought in the under-48 kg category.

Getting started

Many people start to learn judo when they are at school. They join a small club that meets once or twice a week to practise, and sends fighters to competitions and grading exams. Once the fighter becomes more interested in the sport and wants more practice, he or she may join a bigger club with better training facilities and higher level coaching.

Clothing and equipment

Judo gear is relatively simple. The full judo outfit is known as *gi*. For male fighters it is made up of a jacket and trousers made of strong cotton or a similar fabric, plus a strong belt that ties around the outside of the jacket. The belt's colour and markings show what grade the fighter has reached. Female fighters also wear a white leotard or T-shirt (which must be long enough to be tucked right into their trousers). No shoes are worn.

The other main piece of equipment is the *tatami* – the mat on which practice and competition take place. The *tatami* is used to limit the fighting area and to cushion the impact of falling. In competitions it must be at least 8 metres square, with a 1-metre danger area and a 3-metre safety zone outside it. However, smaller *tatami* are used for practice.

Temporary and permanent *dojos*

Many smaller judo clubs have their *dojo* in a space they share with other people – a school sports hall or community centre, for example. This means that after each session the *tatami* must be cleared away and the space left free for others to use. As judo grows in popularity, however, there are increasing numbers of permanent *dojo*, where practice facilities are available all the time. These *dojo* often have highly experienced teachers, who are often top-level fighters able to pass on advice to promising youngsters.

These young judo students are learning their first throws as their coach stands in the background, checking that everything is being done correctly.

Training groups

At the *dojo*, people practise together in groups of up to twenty, with one teacher explaining and watching what they do. Every fighter works with a training partner. First they practise the technique they are learning, then they become an opponent for the other person to practise on. It is important that everyone treats their training partner with respect, as without them it would not be possible to learn.

This group of judo students are watching a demonstration of a new technique. Afterwards they will split into pairs to practise the move – first one letting himself be thrown, then the other.

Safety fact

Judo belts must always be knotted at the front, to prevent injuries to the spine caused by falling on the knot.

How to tie a judo belt

Judo belts have to be tied in a very specific way:

1) Place the very middle of the belt on your stomach. Loop both ends behind you and bring them back to the front.
2) Cross the right end over the left end, then thread it up and under both loops, in the middle of your stomach.
3) Cross the left end over the right end and tie them tightly together. Both ends should be equal length.

Judo structure

When beginners join a judo club, they get a licence and membership of their national judo organization. The licence allows them to take part in grading exams and to enter competitions. Fighters who have only just started to learn judo wear a white belt. As they become more skilful they earn different coloured belts by taking examinations (see pages 40–41).

Judo ranks

The colour of belt that junior fighters are allowed to wear varies from country to country. In many places, juniors have eighteen grades, called *mon*. The belt order is white, yellow, orange, green, blue and brown. Each belt can have one, two or three red bars sewn onto it – three bars is a higher *mon* than one.

Seniors (usually aged sixteen and over) have ten grades, called *kyu*. Reaching the tenth *kyu* allows you to wear a black belt. The tenth *kyu* is divided into ten further grades, called *dan*. First to fifth *dan* fighters wear a black belt, which they can carry on wearing right through to tenth *dan* if they like. However, if they choose to, they can instead wear a red-and-white blocked belt from sixth to eighth *dan*, and a red belt at ninth or tenth *dan*.

Scoring in competitions

In competition, fighters win (or advance to the next round) in one of three ways. Scoring either a single *ippon* or two *waza-ari* (see panel on page 11) will win the contest outright. If neither fighter manages this, points are added up from the *waza-ari*, *yuko* and *koka* each fighter has scored. One *waza-ari* beats all *yuko*, and one *yuko* beats all *koka*. So no fighter can lose to an opponent who has scored lots of points, but at a lower grade.

Here, a groundwork technique is being demonstrated to a group of students. Watching a more experienced, higher-rank judo fighter is the first step in learning new skills.

Judo scoring categories

The judges indicate scores in the bout using a system of coloured flags. Usually there is a referee on the *tatami* with the fighters, plus two other judges nearby. There are four different categories of score in judo competition:

Ippon
i) a throw where the opponent lands with force on their back
ii) submission from an armlock or stranglehold
iii) a 25-second hold-down

Waza-ari
i) a throw where the opponent lands with force, partly on their side
ii) a 21- to 25-second hold-down

Yuko
i) a throw lacking force or where the opponent lands on their side
ii) a 15- to 20-second hold-down

Koka
i) a throw where the opponent lands on their thigh or buttocks
ii) a 10- to 15-second hold-down.

Weight divisions fact

At senior level, men and women each fight in one of seven possible weight divisions, as listed in the table below. There is also an 'open' division, where fighters of different weights can compete against each other.

Senior men judo weight divisions						
under 60 kg	60–66 kg	66–73 kg	73–81 kg	81–90 kg	90–100 kg	over 100 kg

Senior women judo weight divisions						
under 48 kg	48–52 kg	52–57 kg	57–63 kg	63–70 kg	70–78 kg	over 78 kg

Falling

Falling is the first skill a new *judoka* (the name for a person who practises judo) learns. It is also an important skill for competitors at the very top level. Skill at falling can mean the difference between suffering *ippon* and losing, or *yuko* and staying in the fight. But the main reason all *judoka* need to develop skill at falling is that it helps prevent injuries when being thrown.

Protection

The most important parts of the body to protect against injury are the head, neck and base of the spine. Falling techniques, which are known as *ukemi*, have been developed to help shield these areas from injury as much as possible. Continuous practice of *ukemi* also strengthens a *judoka's* muscles, making it harder for their body to be twisted out of shape and injured.

Protection from injury is also one of the reasons why *judoka* fight in weight categories. Fighting people of a similar weight makes it less likely that someone will be dangerously overpowered by their opponent.

Falling essentials

The essential skills of falling are to keep your head tucked in and your back bent forwards. *Judoka* use their hands, arms, feet and legs to cushion the impact of the fall, rather than taking the full force of it on any one part of their body and thus suffering an injury. These falling techniques are also known as break-falls.

These fighters will hit the mat with a lot of force. Using proper technique to break their fall is crucial if they want to avoid being injured. For this reason, break-falls are the first thing a new judoka *learns when beginning in the sport.*

Training benefits

As well as making it harder for an opponent to score points, mastering *ukemi* can also build a *judoka's* confidence, since they are less afraid of being thrown. This in turn makes them more confident about launching their own attacks in practice sessions, which has a benefit for competitions. *Judoka* can experiment with new throws and techniques in practice, then apply them in competition.

Different types of *ukemi*

Various techniques are used for falling, depending on the direction of the fall. To the back or side, the palms of the hands, the forearms and (for side falls) the outer thigh are used to cushion the *judoka's* body. In front falls, the knees, forearms and palms are used. These are also used to cushion the fall when a *judoka* spins out sideways.

In a forward break-fall, *judoka* roll forwards onto one shoulder and then the opposite hip. Their legs come over practically straight, ideally with enough force to allow them to continue the roll back to a standing position.

This judoka *is executing a backwards break-fall, using his hands and forearms to take some of the force of the landing.*

Ukemi fact

A good way for a *judoka* to keep their head tucked in properly is to look straight at the knot of their belt.

This forward break-fall technique is an excellent way to avoid injury. The force of the fall is absorbed in the roll forwards, and often the judoka *can stand straight up again afterwards.*

The basics

Top-level judo players all need to have excellent balance, especially the ability to keep their feet rooted to the floor even when being pushed and shoved by an opponent. The big throws that make judo such a spectacular sport are the result of one fighter breaking another's balance. It is skill at this ability, rather than power, that usually decides a contest between fighters of the same weight.

Six basic postures

There are six basic postures in judo, each of which is designed to allow a fighter to shift their body position without losing their balance. These postures are:

- natural posture – standing relaxed and upright with feet shoulder width apart
- right and left natural posture – standing relaxed and upright as above, but with either the right or left foot forward
- defensive posture – body upright, but feet slightly more than shoulder-width apart and knees slightly bent
- right and left defensive posture – as above, but with either the right or left foot forward.

The judoka *on the right in this photo has adopted the right defensive posture.*

Basics fact

Right from the start, a *judoka* should concentrate on mastering the basic skills of judo properly. If they are lazy about getting them right at first, every subsequent practice session using the wrong techniques makes it that little bit harder to get them right in the future.

Djamel Bouras of France (wearing the red belt) tries to take hold of K. Savchis of Russia during a bout at the 1996 Atlanta Olympics.

Taking hold

Another crucial element of a top *judoka's* skills is taking hold of their opponent. This is known as *kumikata*. The *judoka* grips either their opponent's body or, more usually, their *gi* (clothing), which can then be used as a lever to try and force them off balance. Normally they grip a combination of sleeves, the side of the jacket and the lapel. Some *judoka* are known for their vice-like grips – one of the greatest ever at this technique was Britain's Olympic silver medallist Neil Adams.

Top *judoka*, such as Kosei Inoue of Japan, practise their throwing techniques again and again, using various different holding positions. In a high-level contest there may be only one chance for them to take a good grip of their opponent, so they practise throws from a variety of different starting points.

Neil Adams (facing the camera) was one of Britain's top judoka *in the 1980s. Here he is pictured fighting for a grip on an opponent. Neil's vice-like grip was famous throughout the judo world: once he fastened on an opponent they rarely escaped.*

Tai sabaki

Tai sabaki is the name given to shifting your body position to stop your opponent throwing you. By anticipating an attack, top *judoka* can block it using *tai sabaki*, adapting their body position and balance to make the throw impossible. It is also possible to move with the **momentum** of an attack, meaning that the opponent cannot get enough leverage into the throw to finish it successfully.

Throws

Just as being able to keep their balance is an essential defensive skill for all *judoka*, so breaking an opponent's balance is a crucial attacking skill. Throwing techniques revolve around catching or forcing an opponent off-balance. They also often use an opponent's own **momentum** against them. Top *judoka* make their throws with great speed and decisiveness.

Kuzushi – breaking balance

Breaking an opponent's balance is known as *kuzushi*. Making a throw in judo depends on a complicated combination of factors. To be successful, an attacker must have good balance and body position, and a strong and well-positioned grip on their opponent. Only then can balance be broken in the correct way to allow a throw to be made successfully.

Different grips on an opponent can be used to break their balance in different ways. Breaking an opponent's balance backwards might make them vulnerable to *ouchi gari*, a throw that would continue their backwards motion. Breaking it to the right might make them vulnerable to *uchimata*, which begins with the opponent moving to the side and down.

Hip throws

Many judo throwing techniques are based on the large hip throw, otherwise known as *ogoshi*. This throw uses the attacker's hips and legs to throw the opponent. The attacker turns inside the defender's grip with slightly bent knees, pulling on their sleeve and the back of their belt. As the attacker straightens their knees, the opponent is lifted and rolled over the attacker's hip, then deposited on their back on the floor.

Here, British judoka Michelle Rogers is using a classic hip throw, uki goshi, to try for an ippon score at the Paris Super A tournament in 2001. Rogers sensed that her opponent's balance was weak and reacted quickly. The photo also shows how important it is to have a good grip!

Shoulder throws

Shoulder throws are often even more spectacular than hip throws. The attacker has to get down low to throw their opponent, and the throw often takes power from the strength of the attacker's bent legs.

In *morote seoi nage* (the two-handed shoulder throw), for example, fighters grip their opponent's right sleeve and left lapel. The attacker pulls on the right sleeve, turning their hand so that the little finger is on top, then steps inside and across with their right foot. The attacker's elbow slips inside too, under the opponent's right armpit. The aim is to end up with bent knees and the opponent's chest locked against your back. The attacker's left hand continues to pull, and the opponent is thrown over the right shoulder.

Kosei Inoue of Japan takes gold in the 2000 Olympic final. He scored ippon *for this throw of Nicolas Gill from Canada. The photo clearly shows how the leverage points of lapel, sleeve and calf have been used to break Gill's balance completely.*

Kuzushi fact

Although photos often show *kuzushi* techniques with the opponent standing still, they are only properly effective when the opponent is moving.

Reaping and sweeping

Top *judoka* can attack their opponents in many ways – the variety of techniques they can use is huge. Among them are reaping and sweeping throws, where the opponent finds their feet disappearing out from under them, swept away by an unexpected attack. These often use the legs and feet, but for some reaps the attacker may use their hands. Each reap, as with other throws, depends on specific *kuzushi* balance-breaking techniques to make it successful. The leg movements alone will not work.

In this photo, Darcel Yandzi of France can be seen throwing Bronislaw Wolkowicz of Poland with osoto gari, *the large outer reap.*

Kosoto gari, the small outer reap, is caught perfectly by the camera in this photo. Slightly off-balance, the fighter facing the camera has had her left foot swept out from beneath her. With her feet so far apart, and one foot in the air, she cannot avoid being thrown.

Large reaps

Large reaps are performed using the leg to sweep an opponent off their feet. The first main type is the large outer reap (*osoto gari*), where the attacker steps inside and uses their right leg to sweep away the opponent's right leg, forcing them to fall to the attacker's left.

For the large inner reap (*ouchi gari*), the attacker steps forward and hooks their right leg around the opponent's left leg. By staying in balance, the attacker is able to lift the opponent's right leg forward. The opponent is then thrown to the ground.

Small reaps

Small reaps are those in which the attacker uses their foot, rather than leg, to unbalance their opponent. In the small outer reap (*kosoto gari*), the attacker's left leg steps behind the defender's right, then sweeps it forwards so that the defender falls over backwards and to the left. In the small inner reap (*kouchi gari*), the attacker uses their right foot to sweep the opponent's right foot out and to the right.

Hips and thighs

Other throws use the hips (for example, the hip wheel *koshi guruma* and the hip sweep *harai goshi*), or the thigh (for example, the inner thigh reaping throw *uchimata*).

Technique fact

The position of the head is crucial in throwing technique. The head determines the direction of the throw, so *judoka* look in the direction they want the throw to go.

Foul fact

Kicking is not allowed in judo, so it is important for all *judoka* to learn the reaping and sweeping techniques well. Otherwise they risk being given a foul by the referee.

Using the hands

Use of the hands on an opponent's legs is popular with *judoka* who use the wrestling style (see page 7). One popular example of this is the two-handed reap (*morote gari*). In this move, as the opponent tries to take hold, the attacker steps forward and grabs the backs of their legs. Pushing the right shoulder into the knot of the defender's belt, the attacker lifts the legs. The opponent is thrown to the floor. This throw has to be made quickly or the defender can twist out of it, since the attacker has no control over their upper body.

Kellie Roberts of the UK attacks with kouchi gari, *the small inner reap. Roberts has stepped inside to sweep away her opponent's right foot with her own left foot. The other fighter clings on, hoping to avoid* ippon.

Advanced technique

Once *judoka* have mastered the basic techniques, they are ready to use them in combination, and to adapt their attacks according to what their opponent is doing. It is this ability to make endless adaptations during a match, often instinctively, which marks out the very best judo stars.

Combinations

When fighting an experienced opponent, one simple attack is unlikely to be successful. Top *judoka* are able to recognize an attack as it begins, and can shift their body weight to block it. Sometimes an attacker can use this blocking movement as the start of a new attack, making it possible for them to throw the defender in a different way. This is known as a combination. The best competitors may perform several **feints** until they feel they have broken an opponent's balance and can launch a true attacking move. Sometimes the new attack is in the same direction as the feint: this is called *renzoku waza*. When the new attack takes a new direction it is called *renraku waza*.

An attempted attack by El Salvador's Ledis Salazar (in white) has failed, leaving her off-balance. Karina Bryant of Great Britain (in blue) takes instant advantage, using the momentum of the attack to throw her opponent to the floor.

Counters

In competition judo, the rules say that both fighters must have an attacking attitude. Those who are seen as too defensive risk being penalized by the referee. But this does not mean that they must both be launching new attacks the whole time. One of the key techniques in judo is to use the movement from your opponent's attack to launch your own counter-attack, or counter. The attacker will have had to shift their weight to attack, making it possible for their balance to be broken more easily.

Practice fact

The best way to develop competition skills is in a free-practice session, known as *randori*. This is where *judoka* split into pairs for mini-bouts in which they can attempt combinations and counters, among other things. There is no referee so they must work together, under the eyes of their coach.

Ryoko Tamura and 'Yawara'!

Ryoko Tamura is a legendary figure in Japan. She has even had a comic strip, 'Yawara', modelled on her. Despite being tiny, even for the under-48 kg division, she has won five world titles. After two Olympic silver medals (in 1992 and 1996) she finally won gold at the Sydney Olympics in 2000. Tamura is famous for her incredibly fast technique, which often takes opponents unawares.

Sacrifices

Sacrifices are when *judoka* appear to allow themselves to be put in a weak position, only to turn it to their own advantage. Usually this means that they go down on their back or side in order to throw their opponent using their feet and body movement. This is fun for beginners to practise and gives a spectacular result, like something out of an action film! But against experienced opponents sacrifices are risky unless they are done extremely well, because the person performing them starts from a position of disadvantage.

Sacrifices are most commonly used by wrestling-style fighters: their style of judo makes them more naturally comfortable fighting on the *tatami*. The contrast of styles when a traditional fighter meets a wrestling fighter can make for interesting tactics from both sides.

Groundwork

Although not as spectacular to untrained observers as throws, groundwork is equally important. Top-level competitors such as John Buchanan of the UK have to be as strong at groundwork as everything else. This can give them the confidence to attempt throws, since they know that if the throw is unsuccessful or only partially successful they will be able to continue the attack on the ground.

The fighter on top in this photo is employing kesa gatame, *also known as the scarf hold because the opponent's neck is wrapped up like a scarf!*

Throws to holds

The best *judoka* are able to make some throws with the possible aim of turning them into a hold on the ground. This means that even if the throw doesn't score *ippon*, it can still lead to a strong groundwork position and the possibility of more points or victory. This change is called transition.

Hold-downs

Hold-downs (in Japanese, *osaekomi waza*) are techniques where the opponent is pinned to the ground, usually on their back. Referees announce *osaekomi* when they think the following have happened:

• The attacker has their body in one of two approved positions.

• The defender is under the control of the attacker and has one or both shoulders plus the back in contact with the mat.
• The attacker's legs or body are not being controlled by the defender's legs.
• At least one of the contestants has part of their body within the competition area.

Once the referee has called *osaekomi*, the countdown begins. If the hold remains in place for 25 seconds, *ippon* is scored and the contest is over.

The fighter on top here has wrapped up his opponent in *yoko shiho gatame, otherwise known as the side-locking four-corner hold, for obvious reasons!*

Armlocks

Top *judoka* will sometimes be able to fight back from a hold-down using an armlock. Armlocks (*kansetsu waza*) are techniques in which pressure is put on an opponent's elbow joint in order to force a submission. There are other *kansetsu waza* in judo, but only those applied to the elbow are allowed in competition.

Groundwork points

Groundwork is important because it can win a contest or extra points.

- A 25-second hold-down wins the contest with *ippon*.
- A 21- to 25-second hold-down scores *waza-ari*.
- A 15- to 20-second hold-down scores yuko.

Bridging fact

Bridging is one of the most common escapes from a hold. Using mainly their leg and back muscles, as well as their arms, *judoka* lift their hips off the floor.

The effect is to roll their attacker off or push them away. At the very least, they can stop their back from being in contact with the ground, breaking the hold temporarily.

Warming up and stretching

In judo even a top-level *judoka* is likely to find their body being bent out of shape and subjected to very unusual stresses and strains. This makes the warming-up process even more important than in most sports. *Judoka* also find **flexibility** helpful, as it allows them to twist their bodies with greater ease.

Warming up

Warming up properly before starting hard judo practice or competition is crucial. It is important to warm up progressively, starting relatively slowly. Judo coaches make sure their *judoka* warm up four main categories of muscles: the legs; the abdominal belt; the shoulders, chest and arms; and the upper back and neck.

A few useful warm-up stretches are explained on the right, but there are many more. A *judoka* should never perform a stretch unless they have seen it demonstrated and know how to do it properly. They should never keep a stretch going until it hurts, as this risks injury. Instead, they should just hold it at the moment when it becomes slightly uncomfortable, then breathe deeply from the stomach to relax.

- Thigh stretch – this is done standing, keeping the hips level and pulling the heel of one foot up to the bottom. The exercise is then repeated with the other foot.

- Back/shoulder stretch – the elbow of one arm is pulled up behind the head, so that the forearm points down the spine. This is then repeated with the other arm.

- Side stretches – the *judoka* stands with their feet just over shoulder-width apart and one hand on their hip. They then bend to that side, stretching their other arm over their head and leaning to the side.

- Neck rolls – the head is tipped to the left, then rolled down so the chin is on the chest, then tipped back up to the right. This is then repeated in the opposite direction. NB: the head should *never* be rolled backwards.

Ryoko Tamura of Japan stretches during a training session at the 2000 Sydney Olympics.

Flexibility is vital if a judoka is to avoid being held down and losing points during competition.

Craig Fallon

One fighter famed for using his flexibility to escape from dangerous situations is the young British *judoka* Craig Fallon (pictured here nearest the camera). In 2002 Fallon won the British title and gold at the Commonwealth Games. But one of his greatest successes – one that put him third in the European rankings – came at the Paris Super A tournament in 2003. There, Fallon managed to escape from an *uchimata* throw by his Korean opponent in the final's first exchange, twisting through the air and landing on his feet. Had the throw been successful, the final would have been lost. As it was, Fallon survived and went on to win one of judo's most prestigious gold medals.

Flexibility

Increased flexibility is helpful to almost all sportspeople. To develop this, they need to follow a regular routine of stretching exercises – ideally daily – in order to make sure their muscles are loose. This is because loose muscles allow limbs to move more freely than would otherwise be the case. *Judoka* find that flexibility of their neck, back, shoulder, waist and hip muscles helps them develop their techniques.

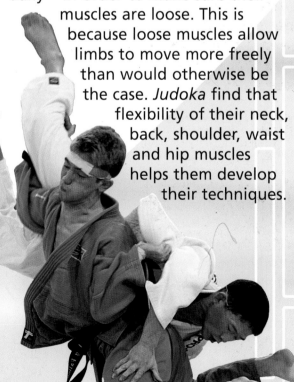

Physical conditioning

Like all top-level sportspeople, international-standard *judoka* need to be extremely fit. Their contest bouts last 5 minutes, which may not sound very long but these are 5 minutes in which a lot of very **concentrated** activity takes place. In addition, a *judoka* has to go through up to six bouts in a few hours to reach a final. Finally, the need for fitness is even greater in competitions known as *kohaku*, in which the winner stays on the mat until defeated.

This illustration shows the most important muscle groups used in judo. Top fighters need to maintain good overall fitness, however.

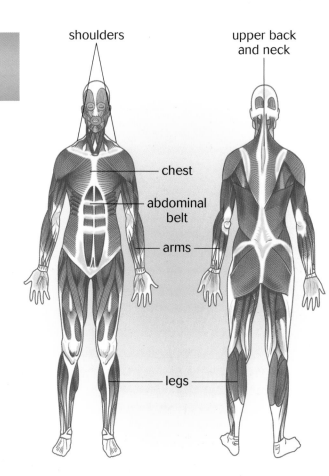

shoulders

upper back and neck

chest

abdominal belt

arms

legs

Using different muscles

Judo uses four main groups of muscles:

- the abdominal belt
- the upper back and neck
- the shoulders, chest and arms
- the legs.

As well as building fitness, *judoka* aim to build power in these areas. They also aim to increase their muscle **reaction time**, to allow faster techniques.

Body-weight training

Most young *judoka* are asked by their coaches not to use weights until their bodies have finished growing. Using weights before then can lead to serious injury, sometimes long-term, as muscles build up too much power for the bones growing around them. Instead, coaches encourage the use of body-weight training – sit-ups, push-ups, squat thrusts, etc. This also provides excellent training for top *judoka*.

Weight training

Later on in their careers, many *judoka* use weight training to develop power and stamina. Some use free weights, but the majority today use multi-gym machines, since the risk of injury on these is usually far less than with free weights.

Sit-ups are a good way for young judoka to exercise without damaging their bodies.

Increasing reaction times

The best way of increasing the speed with which a technique can be used is repetition. Top *judoka* may practise a particular move several hundred times a day, every day, as a way of programming the muscles to repeat the move automatically.

The role of a team physiotherapist

Top *judoka* are accompanied to many of their international contests by a physiotherapist. The physiotherapist's jobs include:

- Checking that the whole team is healthy before they leave for the competition, and that no one is carrying an injury that will stop them fighting.
- Assessing and, if possible, treating injuries that happen in competition. Serious injuries mean a fighter must withdraw, but minor injuries to fingers, for example, can be taped up.

Injury fact

Most injuries picked up in judo are to joints, caused by the twists and strains of practice and competition. Fingers, wrists, elbows, shoulders, knees, toes and ankles can all be affected. The first stage in treating most of these injuries is usually a regime known as 'PRICE'. This stands for:

- **P**revention: stopping the injured *judoka* moving about
- **R**esting the injury
- **I**cing the injury by applying an ice pack
- **C**ompression: applying pressure to stop the injury swelling
- **E**levating the injured limb to stop the swelling becoming worse.

Top-flight training

Top *judoka* follow a punishing regime of training, which includes fitness work and technique practice at their clubs. They also head off to special training camps where they can practise against other national-standard fighters, sometimes from other countries. Of course, on top of all this there are regular competitions to attend, not to mention academic studies for the younger *judoka*!

This is Sophie Cox, a young British judoka. In 2002, Sophie won a bronze medal at the Commonwealth Games in Manchester.

Sophie Cox's competition checklist

Don't forget your:
- blue and white *gi*
- white T-shirts
- water and high-energy drink
- jaffa cakes, chocolate and blueberry muffins. (It's important to have high-energy foods handy for competition days!)
- warm clothes for between fights.

Training fact

Many top *judoka* train 3.5 or 4 hours a day, 6 days a week. That's around 100 hours a month, or 1200 hours a year. Put another way, that's around 50 days and nights of the year spent in training!

Diary of an international judoka

In 2003, Sophie Cox of England was a young international *judoka* who fought in the under-57 kg weight division. In the lead-up to the 2004 Olympics, Sophie was a student at the Bisham Abbey National Judo Academy. As well as practising judo, she was also studying for a degree in Health and Exercise. Sophie's diary of the first three months of 2003 give a good idea of what life is like for an international *judoka*.

January 2003

3 January – international training camp held at Kendall, Cumbria, in the UK. Day starts at 6.20 a.m., with a groundwork session at 7.00. Breakfast, then a technique session at 10.00. After this, running at 1.00 p.m., followed by a log-carry race through the woods. Back on the mat by 7.30 p.m. for more judo till 9.30, then off home, to bed!

7–12 January – training camp in Munich, Germany.

24–26 January – Moscow A Tournament. Record: won one, lost one.

February 2003

8 February – Paris Super-A Tournament. Record: won in rounds 1 and 2, lost in round 3, so into the repercharge competition [from which *judoka* can win a bronze medal]. Won first fight, lost second and therefore knocked out of competition. Excellent that Craig Fallon, also from Bisham, managed to win a gold, though!

24–27 February – international training camp, Hamburg, Germany. Just five sessions, but very intense, with top-level *judoka* and coaches.

March 2003

18 March – noticed a cauliflower (swollen) ear appearing – went to doctor to have it drained.

22 March – Dutch Open at Rotterdam. First fight won by *ippon*, but slight abdominal muscle strain in the process. Second fight won; third fight won but armlock by opponent causes slight injury. Semi-final against current world champion from Cuba, Luputey. Scores even at end of five minutes, so into 'golden score' overtime. A passivity penalty (a score given to Luputey because I wasn't aggressive enough) wins the contest for her. Into contest for bronze medal: won it!

Sophie went on to be selected for the European Championships, and won another bronze medal. She, like many other promising young *judoka*, would then set her sights on qualifying for the Olympics.

Learning new techniques

Experienced coaches and *judoka* can spot a skilful fighter very quickly. Such a fighter will show **economy of movement** and correct **application of power**. Their technique will demonstrate exactly what Jigoro Kano, the founder of judo, meant when he spoke of 'maximum efficiency' or 'best use of energy'.

Keeping balance in a competition bout is at the heart of successful judo. Here, the fighter in blue retains good balance, while the white is vulnerable to attack.

Repetition fact

Top competitors say that 'practice makes permanent – not perfect!' They mean that if a skill is not learned properly from the start, it won't work perfectly however much they practise it.

Learning new moves

Coaches try to develop skilful technique in their *judoka* through an understanding of how humans learn new movements. As a demonstration of what this means, think about learning to walk. No baby is ever born able to walk: its muscles are not strong enough and it lacks the physical skill and balance. Yet within a few years almost all children can walk. There are three key elements in how they learn.

1) They see other people walking. This makes a baby understand that walking is possible, and also gives it an image of what it is trying to learn.

2) They start trying to walk themselves. Their muscles lack strength, and their brains do not know how to coordinate the tricky combination of movement and balance, which they sense through their eyes and inner ear. Through repeated attempts, they steadily develop this sense.

3) Finally, babies are able to take their first few steps. The first ones are wobbly, but every day their **muscle memory** and strength increase, until finally they are able to walk without thinking about it.

Judoka learn new skills in a very similar way to babies learning to walk, and for exactly the same reasons.

Stage 1 – demonstration

First, *judoka* see a new skill being demonstrated by someone who is experienced in it. Often the demonstration begins in slow motion, before building up to full speed. This gives the *judoka* a mental picture of how the skill is performed.

Stage 2 – coached movement

Next, *judoka* themselves attempt the skill. At first, their muscles are not used to the movement, and their brain has to exercise conscious control over each step. At this stage a skilful coach is crucial, as the coach can adjust the *judoka's* body position and movement until it is perfect.

Only through repeating moves again and again in practice do judoka *learn to do them without thinking in competition.*

Demonstrating techniques to junior judoka *is one of the ways in which senior fighters pass on their skills. The next step for the juniors is to work on the technique under the guidance of their coach.*

Stage 3 – repetition

Once the skill has been learned correctly, the *judoka* must build up muscle memory, so that it can be used without thought in competition. This comes from repeated practice, doing the same movement perhaps hundreds of times a day until it becomes as automatic as walking.

Timing fact

Timing is crucial in judo: even the most skilful fighter will not be successful with an attack if it is not timed as their opponent is off balance. This is why *randori* (free practice) is so important: it allows *judoka* to develop an instinct for which skills work best in different circumstances.

Eating for fitness

In some ways, a *judoka's* body is like a machine. The demands of top-level competitions such as the Olympics and world championships are very high. A *judoka* has to be able to perform complicated movements again and again, with a minimum loss of efficiency in the course of several bouts. And, just like a machine, a *judoka* runs better if he or she is filled with the right fuel – healthy food.

What food does

The food we eat does one or more of three jobs. It provides materials for building, repairing or maintaining body tissues. It helps regulate body processes such as digestion. And it serves as fuel to provide energy, which the body needs to maintain all its functions.

Balanced diet

For top *judoka*, who put their bodies under great stress, eating enough of the right types of food is even more important than for normal people. Many top fighters take advice from nutritionists (experts in how the food we eat affects us) to make sure that the food they eat includes enough of the various different types (see panel on the right).

A healthy meal is an essential part of any athlete's preparation for competition.

Food fact

Nutritionists recommend a diet using a proportion of food from each of these five groups:

- breads, cereals, rice and pasta
- vegetables
- fruits
- milk, yoghurt and cheese
- meat, poultry, fish, dried beans and peas, eggs and nuts

Fats are also essential but, like sweets, should be eaten in small quantities.

Sweating down

Judoka fight in weight categories – for example, 'under 60 kg'. This means that some fighters are right on the limit of the category – for instance, someone who weighs 62 kg. People have been known to try to '**sweat down**' to a lower category – running, swimming or even going into a sauna, to sweat out fluid and reduce their weight. They do this in an attempt to be a 'bigger' fighter in a 'smaller' weight category. But sweating down is a very dangerous idea: water is probably the body's most crucial **nutrient**. Suddenly losing then regaining significant amounts of water can cause serious damage, as well as weakening the body's muscles and **reaction times**.

Judoka *who use anabolic steroids like this risk being caught and banned from entering competitions.*

Competition day

On competition day, most *judoka* prefer to eat a light meal several hours before their bouts begin. It is best to avoid fats and meat, which break down slowly in the stomach and will still be being digested hours later. They may 'top up' their energy levels with a snack or, even better, an energy drink that will help their body replace lost nutrients.

Banned drugs fact

There are two main types of banned drugs that could be used by judo players who want to break the rules. These are:

- anabolic steroids, which increase muscle bulk and power and can make people more aggressive.
- stimulants, which increase reaction times and, in some circumstances, aggression.

Top *judoka*, like many other athletes, are subject to checks at competitions and in training to make sure they are not using banned drugs.

Competition

Top-flight judo competitions all follow a similar structure. The fighters **weigh in**, to make sure they are the right weight for the category they have entered. Then there is a short break before the bouts begin. Usually, the competition for each weight division is run from start to finish in a single day, so the champion is crowned that evening.

Weighing in

The weigh-in normally begins early in the morning, at about 7:30 a.m. The fighters are allowed about an hour of 'unofficial' weigh-in, to check their weight without it being recorded. Once 'official' weigh-in begins, however, they are only allowed on the scales once – as soon as they step off, their weight is recorded. Occasionally, fighters who have come in a few grams over their weight division have had to shed clothes, or even urinate, while standing on the scales. They do this to knock off a tiny bit of weight before the official recording is made.

Team managers

Once the competition gets under way, the team manager makes sure the *judoka* know when they are fighting and that they are ready on time. This helps the competitors to focus on the bout ahead of them, instead of other details.

Japan's Shinichi Shinohara looks out across the competition floor towards the crowd as he prepares to do battle with an opponent.

Weigh-in fact

At the Atlanta Olympics in 1996, David Khakaleshvili, the 1992 heavyweight champion, failed to reach the venue for the weigh-in. The driver of his bus got lost, and Khakaleshvili ended up in the wrong place. Having missed the weigh-in, he was unable to defend his title – even though there is no upper weight limit on heavyweight fighters.

Warm-up areas

Competitors are not usually allowed to practise in the competition area, even days before the event begins. A separate area is set aside for them to warm up and practise in, and this is normally where *judoka* wait for their next bout. At top-level competitions like the Olympics and world championships, these warm-up areas have TV screens on which *judoka* can watch the bouts that are going on as they wait. This can be a good way to discover the favourite moves of the *judoka* they may be fighting in the next round!

Competition structure

To win a tournament a *judoka* has to win all their bouts. But losers can still come back into the competition if the person they lost to makes it to the semi-final. This allows them to join the contest for third place and a bronze medal.

Showing respect

Respect for your opponent is an important part of judo – that is why competitors bow to each other after a match. There was controversy at the 2003 world championships in Japan, however, as several competitors were reprimanded by officials for behaviour against the rules of judo. One Egyptian *judoka* was forced to make his bow three times after being defeated, as he hadn't done it correctly the first or second time. Trouble also erupted (below) when a Japanese fighter was suspected of adding detergent to the sleeves of his *gi* to make it more slippery for his opponents to grip!

Tactics

There are a variety of factors that influence how *judoka* approach a competition. Their training, fitness, skill, previous experience and style of fighting, for example, all have an impact on how they will perform. As well as all these factors, *judoka* must consider their tactics for a bout. Will they fight with all-out aggression like the great French *judoka* Cécile Nowak, perhaps aiming to score *ippon*? Or will they be more cautious and try to be awarded several smaller scores?

Changing tactics

As well as planning in advance, the best *judoka* are able to change their tactics to fit the circumstances they are in. For example, a *judoka* with only a few seconds left to score *ippon* is more likely to attempt aggressive throws than a *judoka* who is leading with *waza-ari* and *yuko*. Tactics in or near the red area at the edge of the *tatami* – called the 'danger zone' – will be different from near the centre.

Attack and counter-attack

Some *judoka* rely on using their own technique to move their opponent off-balance. Others wait for the opponent to move off-balance before making a crucial move. The best fighters can shift between aggression and reaction, leaving their opponent uncertain of what to expect.

Strangleholds such as this one are strictly controlled in competition judo, because of the risk of serious injury involved in using such techniques.

Tactical variables

There are many things that can affect a *judoka's* tactics. Being confident at groundwork may mean a fighter is less worried about being thrown or making sacrifices (see page 21). Once on the ground they know they will have a good chance of scoring points.

Older *judoka* may use their competition experience to wait for the moment to launch a decisive attack, rather than making several **feints**. Someone facing an unusually aggressive fighter might decide to concentrate on keeping their balance strong and counter-attacking.

The advice of a coach is important in preparing tactics. Training drills are used to develop tactical ability. Coping with the fighting styles of different opponents (left- or right-sided, wrestling, defensive, offensive, etc.), fighting while behind or ahead on the scoreboard, competing when injured or sick, and any other imaginable situations are all covered in training.

Know your opponent

In top-flight judo, it pays to know your opponent. In the past, eastern European coaches in particular kept detailed files on all the *judoka* that their fighters might meet in competition. For example Neil Adams, a former international judo star from Britain, was amazed to find that **Eastern-bloc** coaches had thick files full of information about him. This type of research into possible opponents, identifying their strengths, favourite throws and weaknesses, has become more common throughout the world of top-level judo.

Cécile Nowak

Cécile Nowak of France (right) was known throughout her career as one of the most aggressive fighters around. In 1989 she won her first European title, going on to win it again in 1990, 1991 and 1992. Amazingly, her first three European titles were won in final bouts against the same woman, England's Karen Briggs. The crowning moment in Nowak's career came when she defeated Ryoko Tamura of Japan (see page 21) to win the 1992 Olympic gold medal.

Major competitions

Judo is a popular sport all round the world, played in almost every country. This means there are always competitions going on somewhere, at some time. Most are small local tournaments. But there are some competitions that all top *judoka* have circled on their calendar, sometimes years in advance. These are the big events that top fighters hope they will one day win.

The Olympics

This is the competition all sportspeople want to win more than any other. Held once every 4 years, Olympic competitions are extremely challenging. Only the very best *judoka* win an Olympic medal of any colour.

In most competitions, all fights in a particular weight division usually take place on one day. In the Olympics, however, weight divisions may be contested over 2 days. This gives the fighters more time to recover between bouts.

World championships

Held in a different location every other year, the world championships are number two on the tick-list of all top-level *judoka*. During the championships, the top fighters in the world gather together to show who is the best.

Regional championships

Different regions also stage their own championships. For example, each year there is a European championship open only to *judoka* registered in Europe. The standard of these regional championships varies from place to place, though the championships in Asia, Europe and North America are normally of a very high standard.

Olympic competition is the fiercest of all. Here, the Belgian fighter Ulla Werbrouck throws Yoko Tanabe of Japan at the Atlanta Olympic Games in 1996.

International tournaments

There are also regular international tournaments open to top *judoka* from around the world. In Europe, for example, there are three 'Super A' competitions each year, held in Moscow (Russia), Paris (France) and Hamburg (Germany).

The Super A tournaments are recognized as among the most competitive events in the world. Top *judoka* with Olympic- and world-championship experience come from roughly 40 different countries to fight in the Super A contests. As well as internationally established athletes, there are always new faces on the scene hoping to prove themselves. Top UK *judoka* Craig Fallon, for example, first became well known when he won at the Paris Super A in 2003.

Other A tournaments are used as qualifying tournaments, to decide whether *judoka* qualify for major internationals like the Olympics.

Competition fact

Judoka competing at a lower standard have several different types of competition available to them, which will offer different grades of opponent.

- Closed competitions are only open to eligible *judoka* from clubs in a certain area.
- Invitational competitions are open only to players from clubs that have been invited to participate.
- Open competitions are open to all eligible players.
- Mini *Mon* competitions are open only to players of lower *Mon* grade, usually up to 6th *Mon* but occasionally up to 9th *Mon*.
- Age-group competitions are open only to players of a similar age.

Ki-Young Jeon

Ki-Young Jeon (left) is Korea's most successful *judoka* ever. He won the world championships in the under-78 kg division in 1993, then moved up to the under-86 kg division to take world titles in 1995 and 1997. In between, he won the 1996 Olympic title as well.

Promotion

All *judoka*, from Olympic and world champions to someone who has just joined a judo club for the first time, wear a coloured belt. This shows everyone else how good they are: the number of techniques they have learned, and how effectively they are able to use them. A *judoka* earns promotion to a new rank by taking part in grading exams.

Getting a licence

When new *judoka* join a judo club, they also join their national judo association. In many countries this guarantees a basic level of insurance, so that if a *judoka* is injured while fighting or practising, he or she will be able to get **compensation**.

Joining the national association also gives *judoka* the right to take part in grading exams, where officials assess their progress and award new rankings – and perhaps a new belt colour – if appropriate.

The younger members of this women's judo team should always be ready to listen to advice and guidance from their older, more experienced colleagues. This is one of the best ways for a young judoka *to learn the skills necessary to progress through the grades.*

Grades and exams

Juniors (usually fighters under the age of sixteen) have their own system of belt colours, which varies from country to country. A common one is described on page 10. Senior belt colours are the same all over the world.

Once a *judoka's* coach feels he or she is ready to move up a grade, the coach puts them forward to take part in a grading exam. In this exam, two evenly matched *judoka* have a contest with each other under the gaze of judo officials. The aim is not so much to score points, as in a competition, but to demonstrate a variety of techniques as well as possible. Of course, ideally this will result in a throw that would score *ippon* in a contest! After the contest is over, the officials make an assessment of how well each *judoka* has fought, and whether they have demonstrated particular techniques well enough that they should move up the grades.

Often a grading exam has a second part, where the *judoka* have to answer questions about judo. These questions may be about the theory and practice of the sport.

Grading fact

One of the most important things in grading exams is to have learnt your theory well. Then it becomes possible to relax during the exam and pay proper attention to the referee's instructions.

Young judoka *can gain promotion by beating someone of a higher grade than them in competition. They are then automatically raised to the same grade as the person they have beaten.*

Respect for other grades

Top-level *judoka* always show consideration for lower-graded fighters. They are much more likely to help them, demonstrating a difficult technique, than to use their greater expertise to throw them around. This respect between the grades is an important part of judo, and it cuts both ways. Lower-graded *judoka* must also show respect for the training and dedication that has gone into making another fighter a black belt, for example.

Being a champion *judoka*

Top-level *judoka* get to travel the world taking part in a sport they love. They train with the best coaches, in excellent facilities. Many receive financial and other help from their governments. Some *judoka* are **sponsored** by companies that are keen to be associated with such successful sportspeople, and appear on chat shows and as part of advertising campaigns. And, above all, judo champions are admired by other *judoka* around the world.

Many big-name judo stars get involved in high-profile charity work. Here David Douillet is pictured at the launch of an appeal to raise money for children in hospital in France.

Crab antics

If you put a load of crabs in a bucket, they try to escape. Up to a point, the crabs help each other: they pile up on one side of the bucket, climbing up on one another to get to the lip. But as soon as one of the crabs gets close to escaping, the others stop helping, and instead pull it back down.

Being a judo champion is a bit like being the crab nearest the lip of the bucket. Everyone else wants to beat you; all the others are trying to pull you down. Whatever tournament you are at – whether it's the Olympics or a small local event – all eyes are on you, and every opponent is desperate to win a victory.

This means that a champion *judoka* has to train harder than ever, knowing that if they don't, somewhere out there one of their future opponents will be preparing to beat them. Unfortunately, this pressure comes at exactly the time when training harder becomes more difficult, because of the *judoka's* other responsibilities.

Ryoko Tamura of Japan is surrounded by press photographers after winning gold at the 2000 Sydney Olympics.

Sponsorship

Commercial sponsors usually want something in return for their money. This might mean the *judoka* taking part in an advertising campaign, meeting clients of the sponsor, or making appearances for them at charity and other events. All these things take time from a champion's training schedule.

Life after competition

Once they have retired from competition, what does a former champion do? They can, if they want, become a 'normal' person, getting a job and living like other people, free from the demands of training and competition. Many former champions, though, stay in the world of judo. They find work as coaches, administrators, commentators or journalists, putting their knowledge of the sport to use.

David Douillet, France

David Douillet of France (pictured in the background) is the most successful male *judoka* ever in international competition. He won Olympic heavyweight titles in 1996 and 2000, and the world championships four times. In France he was also voted Sports Personality of the Year. Douillet is now retired from competition, and coaches the French heavyweight team.

Recent champions

The tables below list the men's and women's champions in each weight division at the 2004 Athens Olympics and the 2003 world championships in Japan.

Men		
Weight category	**2004 Olympic champion**	**2003 world champion**
Open	—	Keiji Suzuki (Japan)
> 100 kg	Keiji Suzuki (Japan)	Yasuyuki Muneta (Japan)
< 100 kg	Ihar Makarau (Belarus)	Kosei Inoue (Japan)
< 90 kg	Zurab Zviadauri (Georgia)	Hee-tae Hwang (South Korea)
< 81 kg	Illias Illiadis (Greece)	Florian Wanner (Germany)
< 73 kg	Won Hee Lee (South Korea)	Won Hee Lee (South Korea)
< 66 kg	Masato Uchishiba (Japan)	Arash Miresmaeili (Iran)
< 60 kg	Tadahiro Nomura (Japan)	Min-Ho Choi (South Korea)

Women		
Weight category	**2004 Olympic champion**	**2003 world champion**
Open	—	Wen Tong (China)
> 78 kg	Maki Tsukada (Japan)	Fuming Sun (China)
< 78 kg	Noriko Anno (Japan)	Noriko Anno (Japan)
< 70 kg	Masae Ueno (Japan)	Masae Ueno (Japan)
< 63 kg	Ayumi Tanimoto (Japan)	Daniela Krukower (Argentina)
< 57 kg	Yvonne Boenisch (Germany)	Sun Hui Kye (North Korea)
< 52 kg	Dongmei Xian (China)	Amarilis Savon (Cuba)
< 48 kg	Ryoko Tani (Japan)	Ryoko Tamura (Japan)

Top 10 most successful *judoka*, 1956–2001				
Name	**Country**	**World titles**	**Olympic titles**	**Total**
1= Ingrid Berghmans	Belgium	6	1	7
1= Ryoko Tamura	Japan	6	1	7
2 David Douillet	France	4	2	6
3 Yasuhiro Yamashita	Japan	4	1	5
4= Karen Briggs	England	4	0	4
4= Shozo Fuji	Japan	4	0	4
4= Fenglian Gao	China	4	0	4
4= Ki-Young Jeon	South Korea	3	1	4
4= Naoya Ogawa	Japan	4	0	4
4= Wilem Ruska	Netherlands	2	2	4

Judo terms

The judo terms below all come from Japanese. When you see the letters 'ai', you should pronounce them like the English word 'eye'.

dan
black belt grades

dojo
place where judo or another martial art is practised and taught

gi
judo clothing, usually trousers, jacket and belt

harai goshi
hip sweep

ippon
a decisive score, awarded either for a throw where the opponent lands with force on their back, a submission from an armlock or stranglehold, or a 25-second hold-down

judoka
someone who practises judo

kansetsu waza
armlocks

kesa gatame
a move known as the 'scarf hold', because the opponent's neck is wrapped up like a scarf

kohaku
competition in which the winner stays on the mat until defeated

koka
the lowest judo score possible, awarded for a throw where the opponent lands on their thigh or buttocks, or for a 10- to 15-second hold-down

koshi guruma
hip wheel

kosoto gari
small outer reap

kouchi gari
small inner reap

kumikata
when a judoka grabs hold of their opponent

kuzushi
techniques for breaking an opponent's balance

kyu
judo grade

mon
junior judo grade

morote gari
two-handed reap

morote seoi nage
two-handed shoulder throw

ogoshi
large hip throw

osaekomi waza
techniques to hold or pin down an opponent

osoto gari
large outer reap

ouchi gari
large inner reap

randori
a free-practice session, in which judoka are able to practise their competition moves

renraku waza
a combination technique

renzoku waza
a linked technique

tai sabaki
shifting body position to avoid being thrown

tatami
judo mat

uchimata
inner thigh reaping throw

ukemi
techniques for lessening the impact of a fall

uki goshi
a type of hip throw

waza-ari
a half point, awarded either for a throw where the opponent lands partly on their side, or for a 21- to 25-second hold-down

yoko shiho gatame
side-locking four-corner hold

yuko
a small score, awarded for a throw that lacks force or where the opponent lands on their side, or alternatively for a 15- to 20-second hold-down

Glossary

application of power
how a *judoka* uses their own strength and the strength of their opponent when practising different judo techniques

compensation
a payment made to make up for something difficult or bad that has happened

concentrated
intense or especially heavy

demonstration sport
a sport that is being tried out at the Olympics or another competition, with a view to including it in the next games. The winners in demonstration sports are not awarded full Olympic medals.

Eastern bloc
a group of countries in central and eastern Europe, including Poland, Czechoslovakia, East Germany, Hungary and Albania, that were governed by communist rulers until the late 1980s

economy of movement
describes the ability to perform an action in the most efficient way possible

feints
pretend attacks, often designed to draw an opponent into making a move

flexibility
the ability to stretch muscles

momentum
forward movement

muscle memory
the ability to reproduce a movement properly without thinking about it, because it has been practised so many times already

nutrient
substance that nourishes the growth or recovery of a living thing

reaction time
the amount of time it takes a person to react to physical or mental demands. A fighter who responds quickly to an attack, for example, has quick reaction times.

Soviet bloc
countries in the former Soviet Union, including Russia, and those in the 'Eastern bloc'

sponsored
paid or given other rewards for taking part in an activity, usually in return for publicity. For example, a top *judoka* might be sponsored by a judo equipment manufacturer.

sweating down
using high temperatures to lose moisture (and therefore weight) from the body through sweating. Some *judoka* do this to make sure they are light enough to compete in their chosen weight division.

weigh-in
when a *judoka* is weighed before competing in a judo match, to make sure they are not too heavy for their chosen weight division

Resources

Further reading

Some of the books below are now quite old and may be out of print, but they should still be available in some libraries.

Get Going! Martial Arts: Judo, Neil Morris (Heinemann Library, 2001)
This book looks at how and where judo began and explains what you'll need to take part. It also looks at how you can practise the sport safely.

Judo: the Essential Guide to Mastering the Art, Alex Butcher (New Holland, 2001)
A book for adults, but with especially clear photographs of different techniques.

Junior Judo, Mike Leigh (Foulsham, 1996)
This book introduces the basics of judo to younger fighters.

Martial Arts: Judo, Barnaby Chesterman and Bob Willingham (Raintree, 2003)
This book provides a brief history of the sport as well as looking at its moves, disciplines and grading systems.

Sports Skills: Judo, Norman Barrett (Wayland, 1993)
This book combines history with practical advice and details of competitions.

Useful websites and addresses

Judo Federation of Australia
PO Box 919
Glebe
NSW 2037
Australia
Website: **www.ausjudo.com.au**

New Zealand Judo Federation
PO Box 83–180
Edmonton Rd Post Office
Henderson
Auckland
New Zealand
Email: **office@judo.org.nz**

British Judo Association
7a Rutland St
Leicester LE1 1RB
UK
Website: **www.britishjudo.org.uk**

2003 World Judo Championships
Website: **http://www.world-judo.com/en/index.html**
This is the official website of the 2003 World Judo Championships, held in Osaka, Japan.

Disclaimer

All the Internet addresses (URLs) given in this book were valid at the time of going to press. However, due to the dynamic nature of the Internet, some addresses may have changed, or sites may have changed or ceased to exist since publication. While the author and Publishers regret any inconvenience this may cause readers, no responsibility for any such changes can be accepted by either the author or the Publishers.

Index